Let's go to Krabi Thailand

Thailand, located in Southeast Asia, is a beautiful country filled with many spectacular areas to visit and is home to over 1430 islands. It is rich with culture, amazing beaches, jungle, an array of wildlife, and an exciting metropolis called Bangkok, known as the Venice of the East. Thai people are very friendly and adore kids making it an excellent holiday for families!

Krabi is a province on the east coast of Southern Thailand on the Andaman Sea, 800km (497mi) south of Bangkok. It is known for limestone cliffs, beautiful white sand beaches, mangrove forests, offshore islands, and mountainous terrain. There is something for everyone in Krabi.

This **Things to do guide for Krabi, Thailand** is perfect for families and helps you plan and optimize your activities to take in a bit of everything. If you love the perfect balance of adventures, culture, and a relaxing beach holiday, this guide is for you! Included are suggested daily activities, expert tips, and more options so you can swap out activities as you see fit in this customizable plan.

There is a free travel itinerary template on our website you can download as a planning tool. Find it at: www.adventurecampitelli.com/shop.

We hope you have an amazing holiday and enjoy it as much as we did!

ABOUT US

We are a family of 4 travel enthusiasts & adventurers who left our jobs and schools behind in 2018 to travel the world. Documenting our experiences on YouTube and our website, we are inspired to share our knowledge with you in our ultimate travel guides. We receive many questions from travelers looking for advice and insights about the countries we visit, so we created travel guides to make travel planning much easier.

Unlike daunting, long-winded travel books, our activity guides are simple, short, easy to read, and written with the family in mind. They're for busy people who don't have the time to sift through multiple websites or pages and pages of information to plan their trip. The guides easily fit into a travel bag, purse or glove compartment and are loaded with lots of fun family activities. Included is an easy to follow itinerary.

LET'S CONNECT!

Email: adventurecampitelli@gmail.com
www.adventurecampitelli.com

CONTENTS

04	What to know before you go *Making your trip planning easier.*
5-7	Accomodations/Transportation/Food/Cell Phones/Currency
08	Famous Thai Dishes
09	Thai Phrases & Culture
10	Must Have Apps
11-12	Sample Itineraries
13	About Ao Nang
14-21	Awesome Beaches
	• Ao Nang
	• Railay
	• Klong Muang
	• TubKaak
	• Fossil Shell
	• Noppharathara
22-28	Boat Tours
	• Phi Phi Islands Speed Boat
	• Long Tail
	• Krabi River
	• Ao Thalane Kayak
29-32	Temples
	• Tiger Cave
	• Wat Bang Thong
	• Wat Kaew
33-40	Other Awesome Activities
	• Emerald Pool & Blue Pool
	• Krabi Hot Springs
	• Krabi Elephant Sanctuary
	• Huay Toh Waterfall
	• Thai Massage
	• Krabi Town Night Market
41	More Things To Do!
42	Youtube Channel

WHAT TO KNOW BEFORE YOU GO

BEFORE YOU PACK YOUR BAGS!

KNOW...

The current rules for entering Thailand & the re-entry rules for your own country.

This information can be found on the government websites for Thailand and your own country. The website **www.thaiembassy.com/travel-to-thailand/thailand-travel-restrictions** has lots of good information.

KNOW...

What vaccinations are required and recommended.

Rules are always changing so it's a good idea to double check before you leave for your trip.

KNOW...

Where the local hospitals and health clinics are for each area that you stay in.

This is helpful to have written down in case someone falls ill or needs a stitch or two. The emergency number in Thailand is **911**.

KNOW...

What travel insurance is required including health insurance.

Let your insurance company know what activities you will be participating in to see if extra travel insurance is required.

Where to stay

There are plenty of types of accommodations in Krabi, Thailand including hostels, hotels, fancy resorts and AirBNB's. What you choose depends on your needs and budget. Resorts can be reasonably priced and you can often find places with a living room and small kitchen to be able to cook your own meals. Plus the comfort of having a pool to hang out in and an onsite restaurant with a buffet breakfast. In Krabi, we had an AirBnb that was in a resort!

In Krabi, there are 3 main areas where people choose to stay including Krabi town, Ao Nang or Railay Beach. We recommend staying in or near Ao Nang as it has more action, is close to the beach and a good base for getting around to other activities.

How to get around

There are many transportation options in Krabi including:

Car Rentals:
This is the best and most flexible option for driving, especially if you are traveling with your family. A car rental makes it easy to get around, and take all the gear you need for the day. To rent a car in Thailand, you need to be at least 21 years of age, have an international driver's license, and show your passport and national driver's license. You can pick up a rental car at the airport for as low as $136 USD per week plus taxes. We found Krabi fairly easy to navigate by car. There are a few car rental services in Krabi. Call around to get pricing as you may find cheaper pricing outside the airport

Local Buses and Minivans
There's a local bus service that goes between Krabi Airport, Ao Nang beach, and Krabi Town with stops along the way. They leave from Terminal 1 and you can purchase tickets in Terminal 1 or Terminal 2.

Taxis:
Using taxis isn't as common in Krabi, except for longer trips. Some taxis won't even do shorter trips. You will find them at the airport and in places like Krabi town and Ao Nang along the main roads. Usually, the fares are fixed.

Scooters
These are a popular mode of transport and some scooters can carry up to two people so it is doable with kids. To rent a scooter you will need your passport, a deposit, payment in cash (usually between 150-450 Baht (approx $5-$15USD) per day, plus the contact details of where you are staying. Although you don't need to show your driver's license (and you don't need a motorcycle license), you can get fined if you are pulled over by police and don't have your international driver's license. Insurance isn't required but if you crash or damage it, you will have to pay to fix the damage.

Songthaew
Good for shorter trips, Songthaews are pickup trucks with two benches in the back and a cover to provide shade and protection from the rain. They are one of the cheapest ways to get around on operate on fixed routes. You can wave them down along a route and press a buzzer when you want to get off. They can cost as low as 20 Baht $.58 USD per person depending on the distance. Have change with you so you can pay the exact amount.

Tuk-tuk
These are 3 or 4 wheeled open-air motorcycle-type taxis common in Southeast Asia and India. They provide door-to-door service and will even wait for you if you want a return trip back. Negotiate the fee beforehand. If you like your driver, you can always get their contact information for future trips.

Currency & Payment
The currency is in Thai Baht (THB). Exchange rates vary but as of Aug 2022 $1 USD was approx. 36.21 THB. Almost all transactions take place in cash in Baht. US cash and Euros can be exchanged at hotels and currency exchanges. All major credit and debit cards are accepted in large businesses, hotels, and restaurants in Thailand. However, smaller stores and cafes may not take cards. There are ATMs but they charge 200 Baht ($6 USD) or more for every withdrawal, so try to minimize withdrawals.

Health & Travel Insurance
While travel insurance may be covered through your credit card or company plan, likely, it will not cover all activities that you plan on doing. For example, hiking, kayaking, and even boating activities usually need to be insured separately. Plan for the activities you might be doing and insure your family for these. You can always add activities later. The costs are fairly minimal. Don't forget to include trip cancellation and trip interruption insurance as well.

Cell Phones:

You have 3 options: 1) add a travel plan to your regular cell phone plan, 2) purchase a pre-paid SIM card. 3) Purchase an E-SIM card. Option 1 is far more expensive and you will often get a slower connection. You can buy SIM cards at the airport (which cost more), 7-11's or mobile phone shops. You will get a local phone number and data. To purchase a SIM card you will need your passport ID and cash. When you replace your SIM card, make sure you put your SIM card in a safe place and do not lose it! The SIM cards usually come with a holder for your card. The 3rd (newer option) is the e-SIM card which you order online, receive a code on your phone, follow the instructions, enter the code, change the settings and connect to a local network in Thailand. Here is one company you can research but there are others: https://www.airalo.com/thailand-esim

WHERE TO GET FOOD

Supermarkets

The first thing we do when we arrive at our destination is pick up groceries, usually breakfast items and snacks. Krabi has many smaller supermarkets or grocery stores making it convenient to get things like cereal, milk, fruit and other items.

7-11's

7-11 is very popular in Thailand and there are a few of them in Krabi. We often went there to buy snacks including things like fruit and yogurt.

Dining Out

Eating out in Thailand is a fun experience and can cost very little. Known for its street food and local markets, you can feed your family for as little as $10-$12 USD total for a meal. Dishes are often shared and you can buy things like meat skewers, soups, rice or noodle dishes, and fresh fruit. A good tip is to eat where it looks busy, a clue that the food is safe to eat and good.

There are restaurants that serve American style of food like pizza and burgers, but these places tend to be more expensive and not as tasty as eating the local cuisine! There is a Starbucks and The Coffee Club, an Australian owned coffee chain, but the prices are similar to what you would pay in Europe or North America. If you want something more local, try Thai Coffee or Thai Iced Coffee. Coconut ice cream and fruit smoothies are also popular at local vendors and super delecious!

Famous Thai Dishes

Thai dishes are a combination of sweet, salty, spicy or sour. Coconut milk, curry and noodles or rice are common ingredients along with meat such as chicken, lamb, shrimp, or beef and vegetables. There's lots of simple food that kids love. Here are a few dishes we loved:

Moo Satay (pork satay)
Pork satay consists of strips of marinated pork on bamboo skewers, charcoal barbequed then served with a tasty peanut sauce and a white vinegar cucumber sauce. Beef and chicken skewers are common as well.

Pad Thai
The most popular dish!. Stir-fried rice noodles with eggs, vegetables and tofu in a sauce of tamarind, fish, dried shrimp, garlic, red chilli pepper and sugar.

Tom Yum Soup
The most popular soup in Thailand. It's a spicy, sour, and aromatic soup that is served with rice. It consists of shallots, lemongrass, fish sauce, minced fresh ginger, shrimp, mushrooms, kaffir lime leaves, lime juice, and minced Thai chili peppers.

Khao Pad (Stir-fried rice)
This simple rice dish usually contains garlic, egg, fish sauce, soy sauce and/or oyster sauce – and spring onion. Sugar, chili and lime juice balance the flavours: sweet, salty, sour and spicy.

Mango Sticky Rice
Popular dessert of rice that is steamed, mixed with thick coconut cream and sugar, and accompanied by yellow sweet mango, served with extra coconut cream on the top. We absolutely loved it!

Common Phrases & Cultural Etiquette

When going to Thailand it's handy to know some of the common phrases as well as important tips on cultural etiquette.

Sa Wat Dee - Hello.
Kawp Koon - Thank you.
Chai/Mai Chai - Yes/No
Kor Tot - Excuse Me.
Mai Khao Jai (my-cow-jai) - I don't understand.
Lah Gorn (la-gon) - Goodbye
Haawng Naam Yuu Thee Nai? (hong-nam-you-tee-nye) - Where is the bathroom?
A Nee Tao Rai? (a-nee–tow–rye) - How much is this?

Cultural Etiquette:

Don't point your feet at someone or raise them higher than someone's head. The bottoms of your feet are dirty and it's considered rude to show them to someone or use them to point. As a rule of thumb, **Don't point at people period.**

Don't lose your temper. Displaying strong emotions is frowned upon in Thailand. Keep your cool even if things go wrong.

Remove your shoes. Common to many Asian cultures, remove your shoes before entering someone's home or a temple.

Use your right hand. The left hand is considered dirty as it's usually used in the washroom, so always use your right for passing objects to someone and for paying.

Utensils - The proper way for eating Thai food is using a spoon in your right hand and a fork in the left to put food into the spoon. The fork isn't supposed to go in the mouth.

Practice your Wai. A wai is a prayer gesture with hands together in front with head slightly bowed. It's polite to return a wai to someone.

Must Have Apps

These helpful apps will help make your vacation in Thailand smoother.

Download Before You Leave

Google Maps or Waze
Either works well for navigation and keep taxis honest.

Trip Advisor
Good for getting reviews of any activities you want to do.

Grab
This ride-hailing app is cheaper than taking a taxi.

Agoda
App to find accomodations. We used this a lot.

MyCurrency
Use this to compare currency exhange rates.

Google Translate
We found this really helpful in Thailand as not everyone speaks English.

wongnai
Find nearby restaurants and other local businesses.

traveloka
Good for booking flights, hotels and activities. There are deals on this app.

Two Week Sample Itinerary

This sample itinerary is an idea of how you can plan your two week vacation. There are even more activities included in this guide to make that perfect itinerary for your family.

- **Day 1:** Arrive at Krabi International Airport (KBV) and head to Ao Nang.
- **Day 2:** Go to Railay beach.
- **Day 3**: The action packed trio: Visit Emerald pool, Krabi Hot Springs and Tiger Cave Temple
- **Day 4:** Take an island speed boat tour.
- **Day 5:** Visit Tub Kaek beach and go to the Krabi town night markets.
- **Day 6:** Visit the Krabi Elephant Sanctuary.
- **Day 7:** Get a Thai massage and go to Klong Muang Beach.
- **Day 8:** Take a Long Tail boat tour to the islands.
- **Day 9:** Hike to Huay Toh Waterfall
- **Day 10:** Hop on a Krabi river boat tour. Visit Wat Kaew temple.
- **Day 11:** Ao Thalane kayak tour
- **Day 12**: A day of two hidden gems! Wat Bang Thong temple + Krabi Shell cemetery (Susan Hoi)
- **Day 13:** Chill at a beach on your last day. Visit Noppharathara beach.
- **Day 14:** Departure day. Have a safe flight home!

One Week Sample Itinerary

If you only have 7 days in Krabi, below is an example itinerary you can follow.

- **Day 1:** Arrive at Krabi International Airport (KBV) and head to Ao Nang. Visit the beach and do some shopping at the market.
- **Day 2:** Go to Railay beach. Get a Thai massage.
- **Day 3**: The action packed trio: Visit Emerald pool, Krabi Hot Springs and Tiger Cave Temple.
- **Day 4:** Take an island speed boat tour.
- **Day 5**: Visit the Krabi Elephant Sanctuary. Go to Klong Muang Beach.
- **Day 6:** Hop on a Krabi river boat tour. Visit Wat Kaew temple.
- **Day 7:** Chill at a beach on your last day. Visit Noppharathara beach.

AO NANG KRABI

Ao Nang is a resort town with a long beachfront along the Andaman coast. This town has access to boat tours and dive sites nearby the many islands off its coast. The town is fairly small and only takes about 30 minutes to walk from one end to the other along the main beach road. There are many resorts, hostels, hotels and restaurants. There is even a Starbucks! We highly recommend you stay in or fairly close to Ao Nang as it is an awesome home base for all your Krabi activities.

There is so much to see and do in Krabi and makes for an awesome holiday for families!

AWESOME BEACHES

If there's one thing Krabi is known for, it's the stunning beaches. Some of the best in the world in our opinion. With soft sand, lush sandstone cliffs, caves, calm waters, and an active marine life, you'll want to come back again and again.!

In this section, we cover 6 gorgeous beaches you and your family with fall in love with. More beaches are covered in the boat tours section.

Ao Nang Beach

- Ao Nang beach is a beautiful white sand beach that is approximately 1km (.62 mi) long. It can get crowded and there are lots of long tail boats that come in and out but it is fun to sit and watch all the excitement.

- The east end of the beach is the best for swimming as there are no boats there. Not a lot of shade so bring an umbrella if you plan to park there for a couple of hours. Don't miss the beautiful sunset on Ao Nang beach!

- Across the street from the beach there are lots of little shops for souvenirs, clothing, beachwear, toys, sunglasses, etc. There are also little laneways running off the main road with more shops that are fun to explore.

- For dinner, there is something for everyone. From Italian to Thai food to Chinese and other Western food, you will find what you're looking for. Our kids are fairly picky eaters but loved the pad thai which isn't spicy and they loved the noodles.

Railay Beach

- Railay Beach is one of Krabi's well known peninsulas and is home to 4 beautiful beaches. There are no cars here and everything is accessible by walking. You can experience it all from soft white sand beaches, crystal clear aqua water, limestone cliffs, caves and a lagoon.

- This beach is south of Ao Nang (connected to the mainland) but due to the rocky outcrops, is only accessible by boat. You get there by longtail boat and tickets are sold at both ends of Ao Nang beach. The cost per person each way is 100 baht (approx $3 USD).

- The boats leave when they are full so if you're there first, you may have to wait a bit. It takes about 15 mins to get there by boat. If you want to explore at least two of these beaches, it's best to get there early.

- You will be dropped off at the main beach, Railay West. It is a beautiful wide beach with small shops, restaurants and bars on the walking street. Activities include snorkeling, kayaking, sunbathing and rock climbing.

- There is a path from the walking street that leads to Railay East beach and takes about 10 minutes. This beach is narrower and home to mangroves and many birds. Enjoy lunch and a drink at one of the restaurants along the beach.

- If you're into climbing, there are climbing schools at the end of the beach. Railay is known as one of the world's top climbing destinations.

- Make sure you visit Diamond Cave, a main attraction of Railay East. It has a wooden boardwalk that winds through the cave featuring cool rock formations and is home to a large population of bats. It has a small entrance fee of 200 baht per adult (approx $6 USD) and 100 baht ($3 USD) per child. You pay this just before the entrance to the cave at a small open office area. It's very cool and you can hear the bats!

- Phra Nang Beach is very popular and you can walk there in about 10 minutes from Railay East along a path that follows the cliffs. It's shorter in length than the other two beaches and has calm, clear shallow water making it safe for swimming. Absolutely stunning!

- This beach is home to the famous Phra Nang (Princess) Cave where fisherman, before going to sea, would make offerings in the form of phallus symbols. There is a large collection of wooden penises that were believed to help with fertility. Definitely a unique place to see!

- The less known beach of the four is Tonsai Beach. It is in between two limestone cliffs and is accessible by Railay West beach by walking around at low tide or hiking over the rocks in the jungle if the tide is higher.

- This takes longer and is more difficult especially if you have small children. Activities here including kayaking and rock climbing. Alternatively, you can take a long tail boat directly from Ao Nang.

Klong Muang Beach

- This beach is located about 11km (6.8mi) west of Ao Nang. It's a wide fairly long white sand beach that is less busy and more relaxing than Ao Nang beach.

- The quieter area of Klong Muang, just outside of Ao Nang, became our home base while staying on Krabi.

- We stayed across the street from Long Muang beach at the Pelican Resort **https://www.thepelicankrabi.com/**. This is a great place to stay for families with a nice pool in the middle and a breakfast buffet!

- It's a great swimming beach and trees offering shade.

- Lined with restaurants and bars, it's also a great place to grab dinner and watch the sunset. These colorful restaurants and bars are located at the north end of the beach and have tables and chairs right in the sand.

- We were able to enjoy a fire performer almost every night on the beach.

- Many Long Tail boat tours to the islands leave from this beach (see more below).

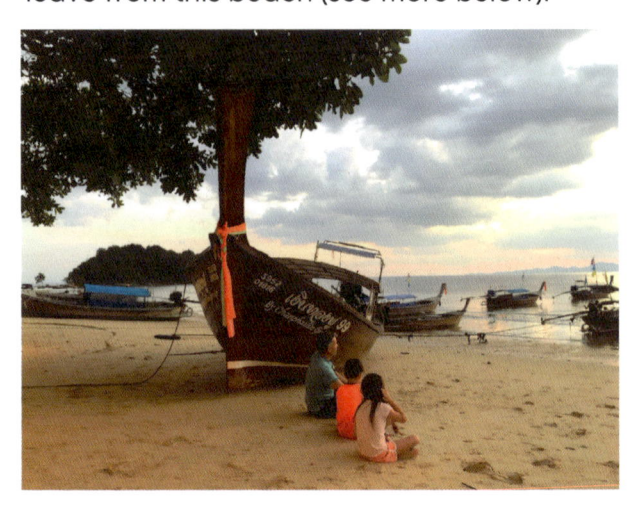

Tubkaak Beach

- Approximately 30 minute drive Northwest from Ao Nang, this is a quiet beach lined with 5 star resorts. This is the place to get away from it all. The long sandy beach has calm warm water and you can wade out quite far in shallow water making it perfect for families with small kids. The beach is quiet and lined with 5 star resorts. It's the perfect escape!

- The north end of the beach is a national park with a thick wooded area. We parked alongside the road as we were not staying at any of the resorts.

- If you're looking for a meal, you can dine at some of the restaurants at the resorts as most are open to the public. There are some smaller Thai restaurants directly on the beach as well for a cheaper price.

- For activities you can rent kayaks or paddle boards here.

- This beach was used as a filming location in the Hangover 2 movie.

Fossil Shell Beach/Krabi Shell Cemetary

- To get to Krabi Shell Cemetery, you'll head back the same way towards Ao Nang beach and drive about 12 minutes west to the beach.

- This is a cool place to see especially if you're interested in geology or historical artifacts. It is said to be one of only 3 shell cemeteries in the world.

- There is debate about how old this shell graveyard is with claims anywhere from 20 million to as high as 75 million years old!

- The first impression of this place is that there are slabs of concrete but upon close inspection, you can see there are thousands of fossilized shellfish and snails, whose creatures inhabited the area millions of years ago.

- The cost is 200 Baht ($5 US) per adult and 100 Baht ($3 US) per child. After 4:30pm there isn't anyone at the ticket booth so you can visit for free.

- There is parking, small shops, and covered areas to sit.

Noppharathara Beach

- Noppharathara beach is a long sandy beach a short distance from Ao Nang beach and much quieter. At only 3.2km (1.98), you can either drive or even walk there.

- This beach is in a National Park and is a very popular spot for locals.

- Being close to Ao Nang it has a similar landscape but there are lots of shells and corals that wash up onto the shore. There are lots of trees and covered picnic tables.

- It has an amazing view and even a lifeguard tower.

- The most beautiful section is on the right side where there are rocks and a bay with crystal clear water.

- Lots of restaurants and street food stalls along the main road to grab food and have a nice picnic lunch.

- Head just down the street to the Ao Nang Landmark Night market for dinner. This is a cool food market with lots of food stalls. It starts at 5pm and goes until 11pm.

BOAT TOURS

When you go to Krabi, you must do at least one boat tour. Even though the beaches accessible from the mainland in Krabi are beautiful, the beaches accessible by boat are even more stunning!

In this section we cover a speed boat tour, long tail boat tour, river boat tour and a kayak tour. All good options for families.

Phi Phi Ilsands Speed Boat Tour

- A bucket list activity is to take a boat tour to see the surrounding tropical islands where you will experience snorkeling in clear aquamarine water, be surrounded by limestone cliffs, and explore soft white sand beaches.

- The Phi Phi islands are a group of 6 islands off the coast of Krabi which takes approximately 45 minutes to get to by speed boat. This tour is one of the more popular tours which includes a visit to the famous Maya Bay featured in the movie "The Beach".

- It is a full-day tour that includes a few stops and a buffet lunch on Phi Phi Don, one of the main islands. This is a fairly large island with lots of restaurants, shops, and even hotels. There is no vehicle traffic on this island.

- Other stops include Pileh Lagoon – a small turquoise lagoon with beautiful white sand which was great for swimming and snorkeling, Maya Bay (viewing only as it is closed for environmental restoration, Monkey Bay (home to a colony of monkeys), and Bamboo Island.

- Along the route you will pass Viking Cave, a cave that houses drawings of Viking ships that were believed to be drawn by sea gypsies. You cannot go into the cave but it is very cool to look at.

The cost is around 1500 Baht ($45 USD) per person. Not included in the fee are the National park fees which must be paid to the tour boat operator. The cost for these is 400 Baht ($12.25) per adult and 200 Baht ($6 USD) per child.

We chose SeaEagle tour and had a good experience. There are lots of other tour boats and different island hopping options as well. If you're interested in this one visit: **https://www.seaeagletour.com/tour/phi-phi-islands-trip-by-speedboat/**

You can also purchase the tours in Ao Nang at ticket booths on the main street Ao Nang beach road or at most hotels.

Note that this tour is quite busy and many people on the boat. It is on a time schedule and can feel rushed but it's nice to be able to take in all the sites.

> **Expert Tip:** Bring a waterproof case for your phone and a dry bag for your things.

Longtail Boat Tour

- Taking a traditional wooden longtail boat is a must-do activity in Thailand! It's much slower-paced, can carry fewer people and is more relaxing than the more crowded speed boat tour.

- We booked a private tour leaving Klong Muang beach to visit Hong Islands, a group of tiny islands with breathtaking scenery. There are soft white sand beaches, coral reefs, and a beautiful lagoon at Hong Island beach. The tour was about 5-6 hours.

- The cost was 3300 Baht ($98 USD) for the four of us plus the National Park entrance fee of 300 baht ($9 USD) per person to visit Hong island. The fee was collected from our boat tour guide who paid the fee when we arrived.

- With a private tour, you decide how long to stay at each place (there were 3 stops). Other tour boats stick to a schedule so there will be times to have the beach to yourself!

- We booked our tour along the street on the same side as Klong Muang beach. Book in advance.

- Lunch was not included, only fresh fruit and water so bring snacks!

- Check to see if your tour includes snorkel gear. We brought our own.

- Hong Island was one of the most beautiful beaches we have ever been to. A calm bay with clear aqua green water, and fine powdery white sand beach surrounded by steep limestone cliffs. True paradise!

- It is a good spot for snorkeling or swimming but watch for jellyfish. The perfect place to relax and you can find shade from the trees.

- If you prefer a tour, there are longtail boat group tours (that hold about 10-15 people) leaving from Ao Nang. Book online or at one of the booths along Ao Nang beach road. The cost is approximately 1400 Baht ($42 USD) per adult and 1130 Baht ($34 USD) per child. The fee typically includes lunch, water, fresh fruit, and snorkel gear. Transportation is also provided. The national park fee is not covered and must be paid at the boat or the park.

Krabi River Boat Tour

- If you want to do something off-the-beaten path, this longtail boat tour down the Krabi city river is for you.

- The day starts at the Chao Fa Pier where you are guided down the river towards the mangrove forest just outside of the city where you will see local wildlife including monkeys and birds.

- The highlight is visiting the famous Khao Khanab Nam Cave which lies between two mountains. The pre-historic cave has stalagmites, stalactites, and statues. You will see a large giant human-like skeleton recently discovered in 2017. Wrapped around the bones of the giant human skelton are the remains of a giant serpent appearing as though they fought to the death. The discovery seems to prove the legends of giants are real! The cave was a hiding spot for the Japanese Army in WWII. The cost to enter the cave is 30 baht ($.90 USD) per person.

- You'll also stop at a traditional fishing village on the fishing island of Koh Klang for lunch at Kanabnam View Seafood restaurant and fish farm. Explore and see how the locals live.

- The tour is 2-3 hours depending on which tour you choose and the cost is roughly 600-800 baht ($18-$24 USD) for a 2-3 hour boat tour.

- Book online or negotiate at the pier for the best price. Online can cost as much as 3030 baht ($91 USD). The online tours include lunch, however, it still can end up costing more. Here's a link to an online tour through Tripadvisor. **https://www.tripadvisor.ca/AttractionProductReview-g297927-d11461241-Mangrove_Boat_Tour_in_Krabi-Krabi_Town_Krabi_Province.html**

Expert Tip: Bring a hat, sunscreen and water. It gets extremely hot out there on the river.

Ao Thalane Kayak Tour

- If you want to do some kayaking with your family, Ao Thalane is a perfect choice as it has so much to offer!

- It's about a 30-minute drive from Ao Nang beach.

- When you start, there's a bit of effort to get to the canyon as you go against the current but it isn't too crazy and is doable by most people. The kayaks are doubles so best that each parent takes a child.

- Tours include pick up from most hotels and there are a few options depending on the company but lengths include two hours, half day, and up to full days.

- There are many stunning things to see including a small but beautiful secluded beach only accessible by boat, a beautiful mangrove forest, and a canyon with tall limestone mountains.

- Winding around the coastline through the canyon, there are hidden lagoons and caves around almost every corner.

- To kayak to the canyon you'll be going against the current so it takes more effort to get there but once there the water is calm and you can relax.

- The half day tour which takes about 4-5 hours is approximately 910 Baht ($27 USD) per person. There are full day options but we suggest a half day with kids.

- Some tours include lunch but if you provided your transportation stop by Khaothong Terrace Resort & Restaurant for lunch. Great reviews!

- Make sure you bring your bathing suit, sunscreen, sunglasses, hat, and towel.

TEMPLES

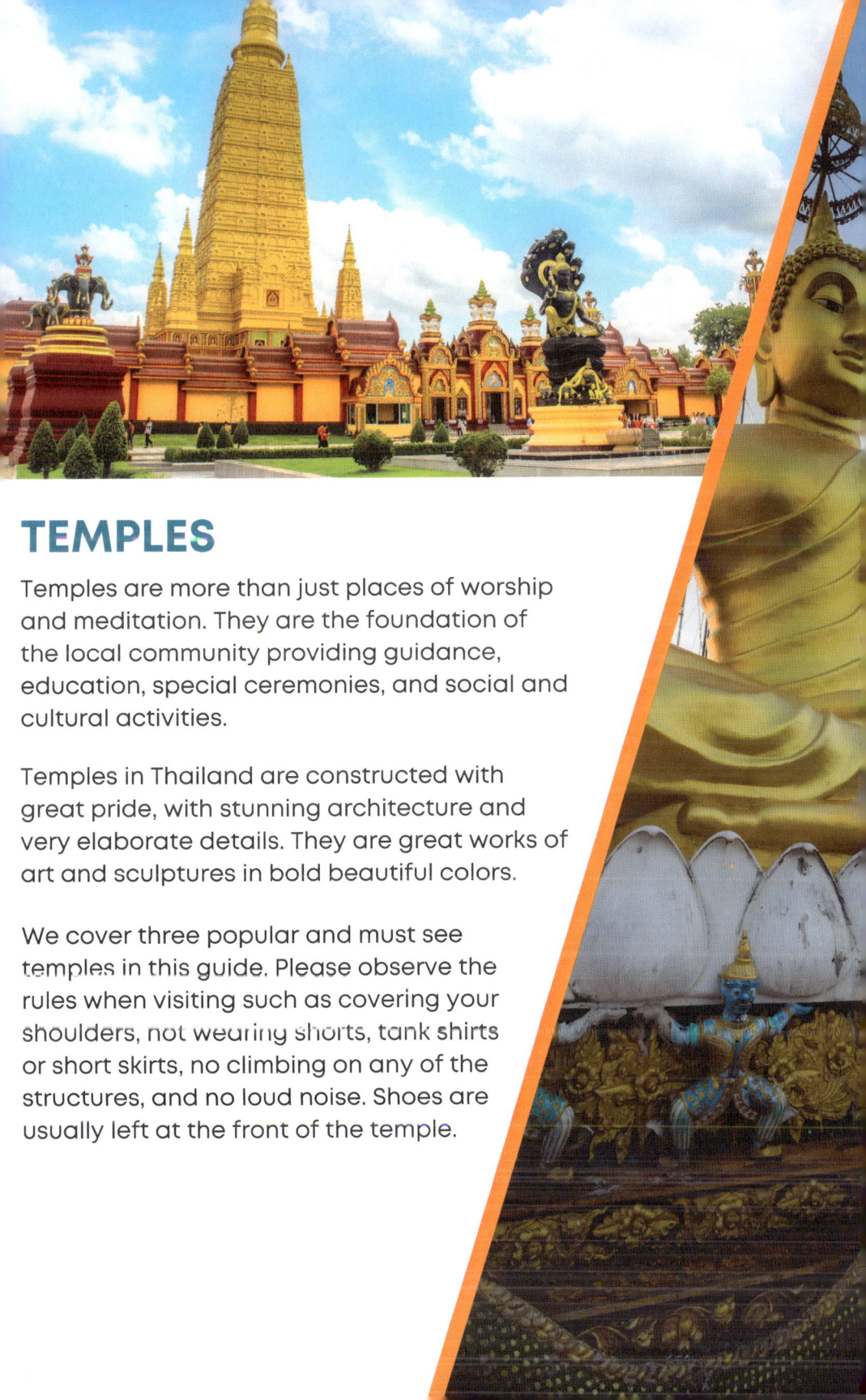

Temples are more than just places of worship and meditation. They are the foundation of the local community providing guidance, education, special ceremonies, and social and cultural activities.

Temples in Thailand are constructed with great pride, with stunning architecture and very elaborate details. They are great works of art and sculptures in bold beautiful colors.

We cover three popular and must see temples in this guide. Please observe the rules when visiting such as covering your shoulders, not wearing shorts, tank shirts or short skirts, no climbing on any of the structures, and no loud noise. Shoes are usually left at the front of the temple.

Tiger Cave Temple

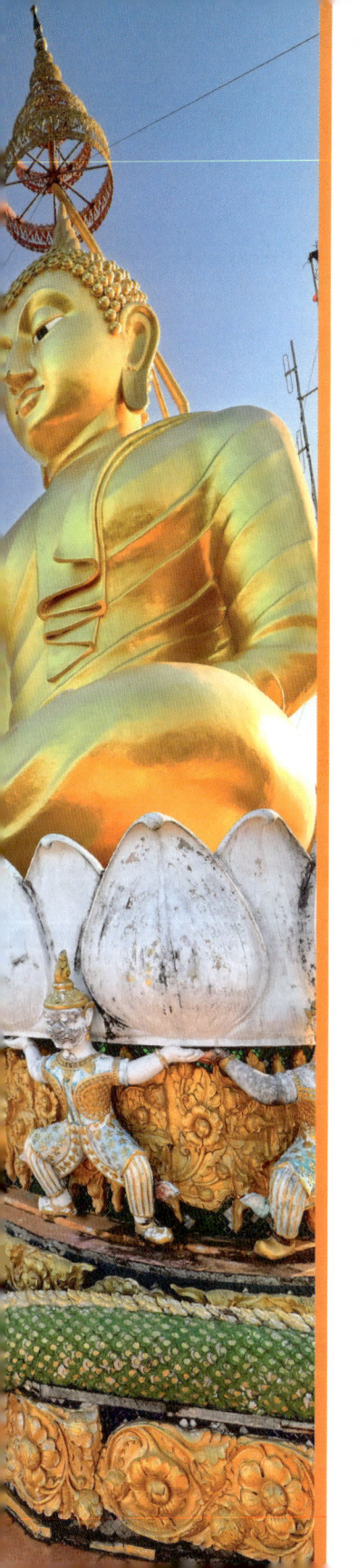

- Tiger Cave Temple (Wat Tham Suea) is a must-see when in Krabi!

- The drive from Ao Nang is just under 20km (12.4mi) and takes under 25 minutes.

- The cave was discovered in 1975 when a Monk went to meditate in a cave and reported he saw tigers. There are supposedly tiger paw prints on the cave floor.

- Monks still practice there and the public can participate in a blessing ceremony. You must cover your shoulders, remove your shoes and explore the cave in bare feet.

- Just outside the cave and down a path you can climb up 1237 steep treacherous stairs to the top of the mountain that has a large buddha statue at the top. The stairs are called stairway to heaven and reward you with a beautiful 360-degree view. There's a sign at the stairs that reads "Pray for your safety".

- If you climb these stairs be careful of the monkeys as they can be aggressive. We didn't have any issues but we saw someone get attacked for their plastic bag.

- Bring water and wear a hat, it can get extremely hot!

- There is no cost to walk up the stairs but you will be asked for a 40 Baht (1.20 USD) donation to enter the cave.

Expert Tip: Dress modestly for the cave. No bathing suits, short shorts or short skirts. Cover shoulders if wearing a sleeveless top.

Wat Bang Thong Temple

- This stunning and fairly newly built temple (under 20 years old) is relatively unknown to most tourists so you'll find it less busy than other temples.

- It was mostly funded by locals and the cost to build it was around 100 million Baht ($29 683 US) which seems very inexpensive for how large and grandiose this temple is.

- This temple resembles a Hindu temple or Mayan or Aztec pyramid but it is Buddhist.

- It has a very wide path and it is adorned with statues of beautiful elephants, monkeys, and hundreds of Buddhas, each with their own name. Its golden pagoda (tower) stands at almost 70 meters, one of the tallest in Asia. It was built to celebrate the 50 years of King Rama 10 since he was a crown prince.

- The walls and ceilings inside have beautiful paintings and statues. This temple is stunning with its bold colors and intricate details.

- The temple is located in Ao Luek, 76km (47 mi) from Ao Nang beach, and takes just over an hour.

- The admission fee is 50 Baht ($1.50 USD) per person and is open from 8am – 6pm daily.

- Don't skip seeing this temple! You'll want to spend a couple of hours here!

Expert Tip: Dress respectively and modestly. Cover your shoulders at temples.

Wat Kaew Temple

- Wat Kaew is the largest Buddhist temple in Krabi Town, but not as famous as Tiger Cave Temple.

- The temple dating back to 1887, is located on a small hill overlooking Krabi town.

- It looks like it's out of an architectural fairyland with shiny white pagodas and colorful walls and ceilings.

- This gorgeous white temple features a grand staircase flanked by golden dragons.

- It is accessed by an entrance plaza off one of the city's main streets called Maharaj Road, near Vogue department store.

- At the top of the stairs you will find the large temple with white walls and dark blue tiled-roofs. Normally the roofs of Buddhist temples in Thailand are red and gold.

- Wat Kaew's ordination hall is very bright with open windows on all sides and features a red ceiling as well as cool paintings on the walls.

- On the temple terrace, you'll find Wat Kaew Holy Amulets & gift shop, as well as food and drink stalls.

- There is no cost to visit this temple and it is open from 10am to 5pm.

OTHER AWESOME ACTIVITES

While Krabi is famous for its world-class beaches, it also has other wonders of nature that must be explored. From elephant sanctuaries to aquamarine pools of water, natural hot springs, and a gorgeous waterfall you will not run out of things to do in this stunning province. Don't forget your camera and bathing suit for these activities!

A Thai Massage and exploring Krabi's night markets should also be on your list.

Emerald Pool & Blue Pool

- There is no public transportation to get to this site so you will need to rent a car, take a taxi or hire a private driver. Another option is to take a group tour that goes to these places. Often lunch and National Park fees are included.

- Assuming you are getting there on your own, from Ao Nang Beach road Emerald Pool is approximately 70km (43.5mi) and takes just over an hour to get there.

- Emerald pool, also known as Sra Morakot, is a natural wonder located in the Thung Teao Forest National Park. We were blown away by the crystal clear emerald water in the middle of the jungle. It seems surreal and is truly magical! There is a Blue Pool a little further down the trail which is also worth seeing.

- The park is open from 8am to 5pm and the cost is 200 baht ($6 USD) per adult and 100 baht ($3 USD) per child. The Blue Pool is open from 10am-3pm. Note that the Blue Pool is closed from May to October due to breeding season of the Gurney Pitta bird.

- At the entrance, there is a security check. You aren't allowed to bring food or plastic items so make sure to leave them in your car. There is a parking fee of about 35 baht ($1 USD) for a car. There is a small fee of 10 Baht ($.30 USD) to use the washrooms.

- There are two trails to Emerald Pool. We recommend you take the longer trail which is roughly 1.4 km (.75mi) long. The shorter trail is about 800 meters (.5mi). The longer trail is an easy well marked path where you see stunning clear mini ponds, streams and an abundance of tropical trees and plants. For bird watchers, there are rare birds here unique to the area. It's a great place for spotting unique and rare animal and plant species. If you're lucky, you might spot the Pitta Gurney bird, which was once considered extinct!

- The natural springs converge in an area known as Emerald pool with clear water matching its name. It is warm bath like water with a mini waterfall spilling into it. The depth is 1-2 metres (3-6ft) and very warm (not hot). Here you can swim so make sure you bring your bathing suit. There are no change rooms.

- The Blue Pool is only about 400 metres (.24mi) further from the Emerald Pool. You take a dirt path to get there. You cannot swim in Blue pool as temperatures can get to 50 C but definitely worth the trek!

- Don't forget to wear insect repellent.

Expert Tip: It's quite slippery getting into Emerald Pool from the wet mossy rocks so wearing water shoes will help.

Krabi Hot Springs

- We suggest you visit Krabi Hot Springs (Klong Thom Hot Springs) right from Emerald Pool. The drive is just under 10km (6mi), 15 minutes.

- Located in the jungle, the hot springs form natural hot tubs on smooth rocks located in the jungle. Water temperature ranges from 35-42C and the water comes from thermal underground springs. The soothing springs are said to have mineral salts with natural healing powers.

- After soaking in the relaxing water you can jump into the river below to cool off.

- There are man-made springs close to the site as well with a place to change as it can get very busy. The natural springs are the best experience by far!

- The entrance fee is 100 Bhat ($3USD) per person and 30 Baht ($1) for a car to park. The opening hours are daily from 7am-6pm.

- If you don't feel like walking the short 500 meters (.31 mi) to the Hot Springs, you can opt for a ride in a golf cart which costs 20 Baht ($.60 USD). Our kids loved the golf cart experience!

- It can get quite busy here, especially on the weekends.

Expert Tip: It's recommended that you only stay in the hot springs for a maximum of 15-20 minutes.

Krabi Elephant Sanctuary
https://krabielephanthousesanctuary.com/

- Getting up close and personal with elephants was one of our best travel experiences! These magnificent animals are beautiful, powerful, and intelligent.

- Elephant sanctuaries are places for elephants that have been rescued from either the tourist industry or work elephants. They often are from poor conditions, and some are abused, overworked, and exploited.

- We learned that it is harmful to ride elephants as it is very hard on their backs.

- There are various programs available of varying lengths ranging from 90 minutes up to a full day that includes swimming in Emerald Pool. We opted for the 5-6 hour program which included a jungle walk, mud bathing, and feeding the elephants.

- If you select a different sanctuary, do your research and read the reviews. Some of the places will disguise themselves as sanctuaries but still keep the elephants in poor conditions.

- You have the option to get picked up and dropped off from your hotel or resort. The sanctuary is about a 50-minute drive from Ao Nang.

- At the end of the experience, you're given fresh fruit and bottled water. There are hot showers and change rooms to clean up after the experience.

- The cost is approximately 2300 baht ($70 USD) per adult and 1700 baht ($52 USD) per child.

- Bring a bathing suit, towel, and sandals.

> **Expert Tip:** water shoes for the jungle walk and mud bath if you don't want your sandals getting completely soaked and muddy.

Huay Toh Waterfall

- Huay Toh waterfall is located in Amphur Mueang in Khao Phenom Bencha National park located 35km (21.7 mi) north of Ao Nang. It takes just under 40 minutes to get there.

- The cost is 200 baht per person (approx $6US). There is a nice parking lot and washrooms at the entrance. The hours are 8am – 5pm.

- Not many people know about this waterfall making it truly a hidden gem in a beautiful lush forest with a stunning waterfall.

- The hike is only 750 meters (.46mi) to get to the waterfalls.

- This five-tier waterfall, cascades down into different levels, each with a pool at the bottom. It's easy to climb to levels one and two but the other levels are much steeper to get to and you may not be comfortable doing the entire climb, especially if you have small kids. Staying at the bottom might be the best bet and you won't be missing out!

- Before reaching the first of the five tiers you cross a bridge over the stream which gives you a good view of the five levels of the waterfalls. You can decide here how far you want to climb.

- Get into the pools to enjoy the cool water and surrounding beauty!

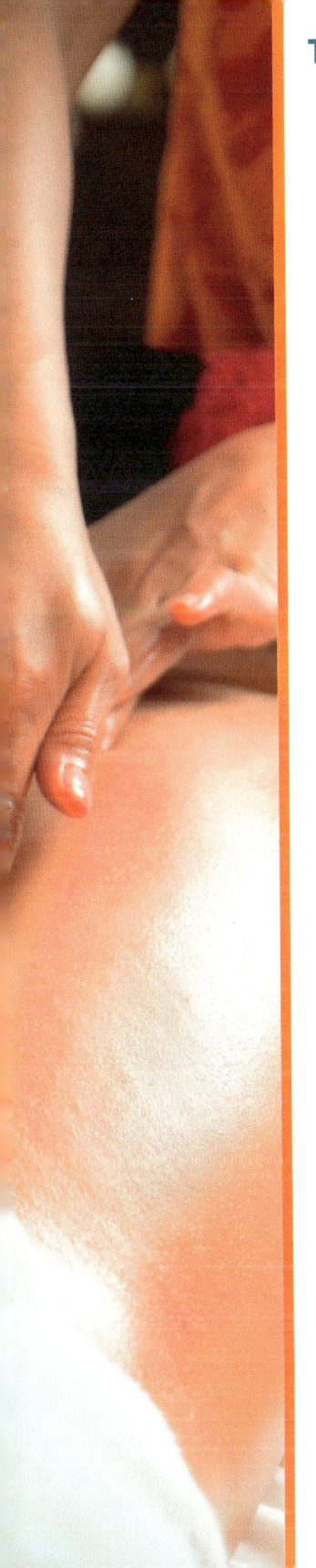

Thai Massage

- Thailand is known for its inexpensive and relaxing massages. There are many places in Ao Nang with good reviews and it's also fun to take the kids. We spent as little as 250 baht ($7.57 USD) per person for one hour.

- It's a different type of massage than you're likely used to but a deeply relaxing experience. For example, the massage therapist will sometimes get up on the table to apply more pressure on your back. They'll also "tap" pressure points and I was surprised to receive a "tap" to the head. Not painful but unexpected!

- Don't worry there's no funny business with these massage places. Just do your research and read the reviews before you book.

Krabi Town Night Market

- The Krabi Town Night Market takes place every Friday, Saturday, and Sunday from 4pm – 10pm. If this day doesn't fall on one of those nights, add it to another night as this is worth checking out!

- The market is located in downtown Krabi in Soi Mharaj 8 in a plaza behind the Vogue department store. Lots of unique gifts, souvenirs, clothing, Thai street food, drinks, desserts, and live music.

- It's usually really busy, lots of friendly local people and makes for a fun night!

- Only a 20-minute drive from Ao Nang Beach Road.

More Things to do In Krabi

If you want to pack more activities into your time in Krabi or swap out activities listed above, check these out!

Visit Koh Lanta for a couple of days

Koh Lanta is an island south of Ao Nang. The easiest way to get there is to drive or take a taxi. It's about an hour and a half to two hour drive from Ao Nang Beach to the ferry and then a 10 minute ferry ride. Alternatively, you can take a ferry from Nopparathara port but it's a much longer trip.

Koh Lanta is much more laid back and the beaches far less busy. We recommend you stay at least two nights so you can do some sight seeing.

Kayak tour to Lot Cave

Lot cave is approximately 50 minute drive from Ao Nang beach. The tour is approximately 2 hours and takes you to a cave with 10 million-year-old stalactites and stalagmites. You will explore mangroves and another 3000 year old cave once inhabited by people that has drawings on the ceiling. Good for beginners!

Visit Than Bok Khorani National Park

A beautiful National Park with nature trails, small beautiful waterfalls that you can swim in and a mangrove forest.

The entrance fee is 300 Baht per adult ($9USD) and 100 Baht ($3USD) per child. You may want to tag this onto Lot Cave as it's just about a 10 minute drive from there.

It takes about an hour to walk the trail. Add time if you want to swim.

Take a Thai Cooking Class

If you're into cooking and want to learn how to make some of the delicious food, you may want to sign up for a Thai cooking class. There are a few businesses that offer this. The Smart Thai Cookery School in Ao Nang got some good reviews. Here's a link: https://smart-cook-thai-cookery-school.business.site/?utm_source=gmb&utm_medium=referral

Disclaimer

The information provided in this itinerary is based on our experiences and research. All costs and activities are up to date as per the publication date of this itinerary and subject to change. Always do your own research, check government websites for latest travel information and choose activities based on your interests, comfort level and ability.

Published August, 2022

Visit our YouTube channel! @AdventureCampitelli

We've created many videos about Thailand including some of the places covered in this itinerary plus videos on things not to do in Thailand
Below are links to a few of these videos:

Thailand 9 Don'ts:
- https://youtu.be/sOugT0Iv9LI

Krabi in a day: 3 amazing sites
- https://youtu.be/-ZlrfGgVM7k

Krabi Elephant Sanctuary:
- https://youtu.be/U1gl7B0-c10

> Don't dream about it **Do** it!

Printed in Great Britain
by Amazon